Whose Woods are These
by Jane Kennedy.

The 49 1/2" x 51" wall hanging captures the serenity of a snowy village in the moonlight. After mastering the technique described in this book you may want to make a larger quilt and add a few new elements to the shattered landscape. Jane has appliquéd the rooftops of a village at the bottom of one of the sections and a moon to light up the night sky. Small trees have been added with thread during the quilting process.

Red Maple, a 39" x 44" wall hanging by Jane Kennedy, catches the eye with splashes of red.

WINTER TREES

JANE KENNEDY

EDITOR: Edie McGinnis
TECHNICAL EDITOR: Jane Miller
DESIGNER: Kelly Ludwig
PHOTOGRAPHY:
Aaron T. Leimkuehler
ILLUSTRATION: Eric Sears
PRODUCTION ASSISTANCE:
Jo Ann Groves

PUBLISHED BY:

Kansas City Star Books
1729 Grand Blvd.
Kansas City, Missouri, USA 64108

First edition, first printing
ISBN: 978-1-935362-13-5

Library of Congress Control Number: 2009929544

Printed in the United States of America by Walsworth Publishing Co., Marceline, MO

To order copies, call StarInfo at (816) 234-4636 and say "Books."

The Quilter's Home Page

www.PickleDish.com

DEDICATION:

To my husband, Jim, Thank you for being proud of my work no matter what the medium and for indulging me.

ACKNOWLEDGEMENTS

THANKS TO...
THE KANSAS CITY STAR PUBLISHING TEAM:

My editor, Edie McGinnis, for her wonderful guidance throughout this process. Kelly Ludwig, page designer, for making these pages so beautiful. Aaron Leimkuehler, the talented photographer who shot the pictures of the quilts. Jane Miller, our technical editor, for her skills in making sure everything works. Eric Sears for his clear, concise illustrations, Jo Ann Groves, production assistant, for her attention to the details when toning the photos. To Doug Weaver, publisher of Kansas City Star Quilts, for giving me this opportunity.

FRIENDS AND STUDENTS:

To Klonda Holt, for being my pattern tester and sharing her work along with the work of Joan Ferguson, Cheri Rabourn, Sande Wilcher and Beth Kurzava. To Rita Briner of Quilter's Station in Lee's Summit, MO. for believing in me and providing a great place to teach. Also, to my brilliant students who have challenged me to "think on my feet" in our workshops. You have all made me a better teacher and I do love the sharing.

TO MY FOLKS:

Dad, thank you for teaching me how to read a tape and to "Draw it up". Mom, thank you for making all of our Easter dresses and for giving me the Singer Featherweight sewing machine.

TABLE OF CONTENTS

JANE KENNEDY

"I have always loved art and have worked in several mediums with Pen and Ink and Watercolor as one of my favorites. After being bitten by the "quilting bug" in 1992, I traded my watercolor palette for a fabric palette and my pen and ink for thread drawn through the point of a sewing machine needle."

Jane's quilts have been part of shows and competitions on local, state, national and international levels. Her work has had the distinct honor of being chosen to hang in AQS shows in Paducah, KY, Nashville, TN, as well as Des Moines, IA, Quilt Odyssey in Hershey, PA, Road to California in Ontario, CA, several Mancuso sponsored shows and IQA Festival in Houston, TX.

In 2005 Jane was asked by the Belmond Area Arts Council to hang her quilts in a two month single artist show at the Jenison-Meacham Museum in Belmond, IA, where she has one of her pen and ink and watercolor paintings in their permanent art collection.

Her art quilts have also been featured in magazines including "Quilting Today", "Traditional Quiltworks", "Quilters Newsletter Magazine", "American Quilter", "$100,000 Quilting Challenge, 2006".

INTRODUCTION

Creating art quilts is such a rewarding process with the vast variety of fabrics and threads available to textile artists today. Fabrics and threads make up the creative palette we use for our art. By altering the colors used for constructing and quilting this project, one can change the look and mood of the piece.

Within this book you will find the techniques used to create a Winter Trees art quilt. The shattered landscape wall quilt is begun by making a pattern and moving step by step through the process with ease. You'll find helpful hints that will smooth your way. While learning and working with this technique, my hope is that you will delight in exploring the possibilities and creativity working with fabric and thread.

-- Jane Kennedy

WHAT YOU WILL NEED FOR THE WINTER TREES PROJECT

Having all of the fabrics and supplies gathered and at hand will allow you to work on this project without interruption or delays. The following is the supply list for this Winter Trees project.

TOOLS AND OTHER SUPPLIES NEEDED:

» 1 Sheet of freezer paper approximately 18" wide by 30" long
» A box of colored pencils, the same kind we used in grade school
» Rotary cutter with a new blade, large cutting mat and a 6" wide by 24" long ruler
» Optional, large 15 1/2" square ruler (used only to square the quilt before binding)
» Sewing machine in good working order with a new needle installed
» Fine straight pins, scissors and a seam ripper
» Neutral gray thread and two bobbins with matching thread
» 1 chalk pencil in a light color that will show up on all of the fabrics, pink works well and will wash out nicely.
» Iron and ironing board
» Spray starch and a spray bottle of water

FABRICS NEEDED:

» 1 fat quarter of a blue or blue/gray fabric for the sky
» 1/3 yard of white or white on white print fabric for the snow
» 1/3 yard each of a light blue, medium blue and dark blue fabric
» 2/3 yard of a very dark fabric for the trees and the binding
» 1 yard of cotton batting
» 1 yard of backing fabric

Pre-wash the fabrics and iron them with a quick spray of starch. This step will make the cutting and assembly of this project easier.

4

PREPARING YOUR WORK STATIONS

CUTTING STATION:

Start with a clean table that is a height that works well for you. This will avoid undue back strain while working on this project. Having a table clear of other projects and paper work will help keep your project on track and organized. Set up the table with the prepared fabrics, a large cutting mat, ruler and rotary cutter.

SEWING STATION:

Install a new needle in the sewing machine after cleaning the lint from the bobbin area and feed dogs. Don't forget to oil your sewing machine. Starting with a new needle at the beginning of each new project will help with the precision of the work. A dull needle will pull at the fabric and put undue stress on the thread and the sewing machine. Fill two bobbins with the neutral gray thread. A quarter-inch seam allowance will be used for the Winter Trees project. So, make any changes to the sewing machine's presser foot or needle position to obtain this. Also, keep some fine straight pins, scissors and your seam ripper at hand.

IRONING STATION:

Set up the iron and ironing board within a few steps of the sewing machine. This will get you up and moving just a little to help curb the fatigue from sitting in one place too long. I like to use a dry iron along with spray starch when pressing the seam allowance in place. Also, keep a small spray bottle of water nearby if a wrinkle needs to be removed. Steam instead of a spray of water will work well too.

HINT: In a perfect sewing world there would be a sacred sewing triangle using the above mentioned three stations with no pedestrian traffic running through. I hear there is something like this in my kitchen!

KEEPING "WITH THE GRAIN"

The importance of keeping the sides of this project "with the grain" is paramount. There are no borders to contain any bias edges on this quilt. Staying on grain will keep the work as flat as possible and, in turn, result in an easier time when quilting this piece.

UNDERSTANDING FABRIC GRAIN

Understanding the grain of fabric will not only help with the outcome of this quilt, but is important in the drafting of the pattern. This also needs to be addressed with placement of the pattern pieces before cutting the fabrics.

Warp yarns run the length of the fabric in the same direction as the selvage, this is straight of grain.

Weft yarns run across the fabric at a right angle to the selvage, this is cross grain. These both make up the grain of the fabric. The straight of grain has the least amount of stretch and the cross grain has a little more stretch. Both of these grains will be used in this project. If handled with care the cross grain will work just fine.

Bias is the angle that is 45 degrees to both the straight of grain and the cross grain of the fabric. The bias has the most amount of stretch in the fabric and is not recommended for the outside edges of this project. Again, there are no borders to contain any bias edges on this quilt top. Avoid the use of the bias direction of the fabric at the outside edges of this project.

HINT: Pre-shrinking the fabrics may help tighten the fabric grain. A spray of starch while ironing will help keep the fabric from shifting as well as make the piecing easier.

WINTER TREES PROJECT

Winter Trees Project

When teaching a class on this project, I have been known to say, "We don't need a pattern." And when I make these little quilts I don't use a pattern. But to help my students grasp this technique, it works best to have the safety net of a pattern. I will teach you how to draft a simple pattern. By the time you finish the Winter Trees project in this book, you probably won't need a pattern for the next one. So, off we go!

MAKING THE PATTERN

Use the 18" by 30" sheet of freezer paper, colored pencils and the 6" by 24" ruler to draft your Winter Trees pattern. There are two colors in the pencil box that are very important and will only be used once each. These colors are RED meaning STOP: STAY ON GRAIN and YELLOW meaning CAUTION: ADD FABRIC TO THIS SIDE.

Set the YELLOW pencil aside to be used a little later.

Place the freezer paper, 18" at the top and bottom and 30" at the sides, on the work table with the dull side up. Using the RED pencil and the ruler, make a line about 1/2" in from the left side of the freezer paper running from top to bottom the full length of the paper. On the right side, again about 1/2" in from that edge, make another line the full length of the freezer paper from top to bottom. Do the same across the top of the freezer paper. This RED line is a reminder to keep track of the grain of the fabric every time a pattern piece is placed on a fabric. Stay on grain.

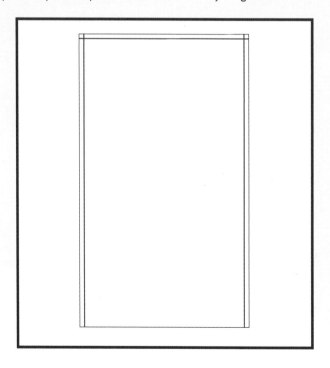

DEFINING THE SECTIONS

With the light blue colored pencil make a reference dot on the right-hand side of the pattern about 17" down from the top. Make another reference dot about 20" down from the top on the left-hand side of the pattern. Use the ruler and the light blue pencil to make a line connecting these two reference dots. This makes the first of the four sections of the pattern. All of these section lines should extend all of the way to the edge of the pattern on both sides.

A second light blue section line should be placed at an angle about 22" from the top on the right side to about 23" from the top on the left side.

The third light blue section line should be placed at an angle about 26" from the top on the right side to about 24" from the top on the left side. To define the sections mark these light blue lines with orange dashes on both sides of all three lines. Put the orange pencil back in the box after you are finished with this step. These are the four sections of the pattern.

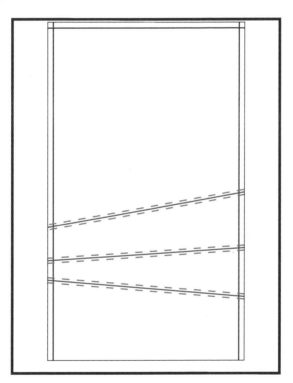

SUBDIVIDING THE SECTIONS

Using the light blue pencil again, subdivide the four sections of the pattern. Working from the left-hand side about 16" from the top, make a reference dot. Line up the ruler on this reference dot to meet a point on the first section line coming in from the left side to about 13". Make a light blue line at this angle.

Working from the right-hand side, make a reference dot about 15" down from the top. Line up the ruler with this reference dot and meet a point about 11" in from the right side on the line just drawn. Make a light blue line at this angle. This will now give you three pattern pieces for the first section.

In the second section, make a reference dot at the right-hand side about 21" down from the top. Line up the ruler with this reference dot. Draw a light blue line coming in from the right side about 13 1/2" to meet the above section line. This will result in two pattern pieces in this section.

No subdivision lines are made in the third section.

Focusing on the fourth or bottom section, work from the left-hand side and make a reference dot about 28" down from the top. Line up the ruler with this reference dot. Draw a light blue line coming in from the left-hand side about 16" to meet the section line. Now working from the right hand side, make a reference dot about 29" down from the top. With the ruler lined up with the reference dot, make a light blue line at an angle to meet a point about 10" in from the right side on the line just drawn. This last section will have three pattern pieces giving you a total of nine pieces.

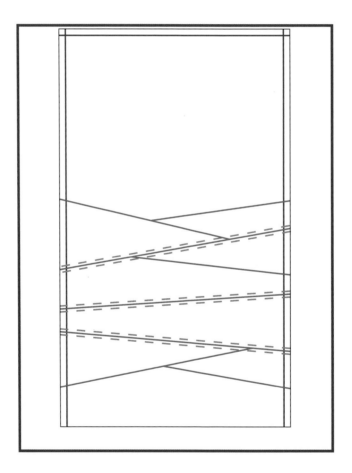

NUMBERING THE PATTERN PIECES

Using the purple colored pencil, number all of the pattern pieces from top to bottom starting with number 1 for the Sky ending with number 9 at the bottom.

FABRIC COLOR PLACEMENT

I have made light, medium, dark and white fabric color placement recommendations on the pattern only to help achieve visual depth in this project. Light colors come forward and add sparks of light. The dark colors recede and add depth and shadows. It would be darkest in the middle of the woods with only a spark or two of light coming through the trees. This creates visual impact in your quilt. Any adjustment may be made to the work if you feel it looks better with the colors and shades of fabric that you have chosen for your Winter Trees project.

- » 1 Sky fabric Blue or Blue/Gray
- » 2 Dark
- » 3 White or White on White
- » 4 Medium
- » 5 Dark
- » 6 Light
- » 7 Medium
- » 8 White or White on White
- » 9 Light

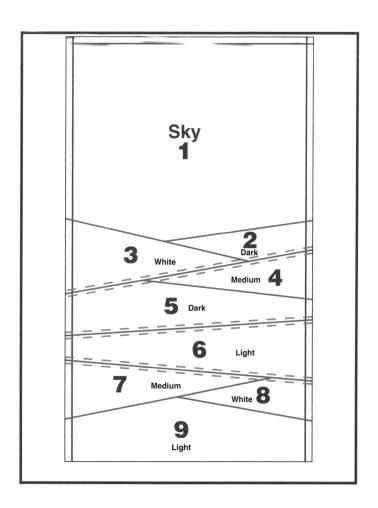

11

SUGGESTED TREES

Suggested Trees are all about the placement within the landscape. The reason they are called suggested trees is that as this little quilt top is constructed you might not like where a tree has been drawn on the pattern. Until the cut is made, the suggested tree may be moved just a bit. Your decision may be to omit a suggested tree all together. A quick audition with a strip of very dark tree fabric will help with this decision if a transplant is needed.

All of the suggested trees should be placed on section lines for ease in the construction of this piece. The section lines are the lines that have orange dash marks. An odd number of suggested trees such as three or five is eye-appealing. For this Winter Trees project, I propose five trees drawn in the pattern. But if an even number of trees looks good then stop at that. Oh my, the freedom to change a pattern! Also, keep an open area, without trees around the middle of the quilt. This draws the viewer's eye into the landscape and makes them wonder what is just beyond those trees.

NOTE: Remember to place the suggested trees on the section lines, the blue lines that have the orange dash marks, otherwise the piecing will result in a Y seam. Putting a suggested tree on another line will also change the order of piecing the quilt top.

PLACING THE SUGGESTED TREES

Using the black pencil, mark a reference dot at the top of the pattern at the left side about 3" in for the first suggested tree. Then at the left side of the pattern on the first section line (the line with the orange dash marks), make another reference dot about 3 1/2" in from the left-hand side. Place the ruler in line with these two reference dots. With the ruler in place, draw a black line from the top of the pattern ending on the first section line. The first suggested tree is now drawn into the landscape.

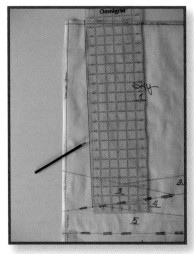

At the top left side of the pattern, make a reference dot about 1 1/2" from the outside edge. On the second section line down, also on the left side of the pattern, make another reference dot 1 1/2" from the outside edge. Connect these two dots using the black colored pencil.

Notice in the drawing a "branch" is growing from this suggested tree. For the branch, the reference dots are placed about 9" from the left side edge at the top of the pattern and down the trunk about 10" from the top of the tree. Draw a line to connect these two reference dots.

Another tree is suggested on this same section line at the right side of the pattern. For this tree trunk, place the reference dots 2" in from the right side at the top of the pattern and about 4" in from the right side of the pattern along the second section line down from the top. Connect these two points by drawing a solid black line.

The "branch" for this tree is drawn using the reference dots placed at the top about 5" in from the right side of the pattern and down the trunk about 6 1/2" from the top of the tree. Connect the two reference dots with a black line for the second branch.

On the right-hand side of the pattern, mark the reference dots for the fourth suggested tree at about 7" in from the outside edge at the top and about 6 1/2" in from the outside edge on the lowest section line. Make the line to connect these two points.

Moving back to the left side of the pattern, make a reference dot at the top about 7" in from the outside edge and all of the way at the bottom of the pattern, make the reference dot about 5" in from the left side. Use the ruler to connect these last two reference dots. All five of the suggested trees are drawn and ready for their root balls.

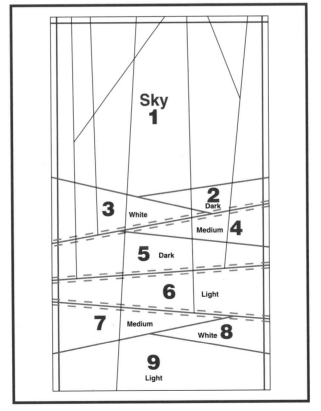

ADDING THE ROOT BALL

With the green colored pencil, make a 1" diameter circle at the base of each suggested tree. This circle or "root ball" if you will, should extend above and below the section line. It is very important to make this 1" circle extend above and below the blue/ orange dash section lines at the base of each tree. You will find it very helpful when it is time to "plant" the suggested trees.

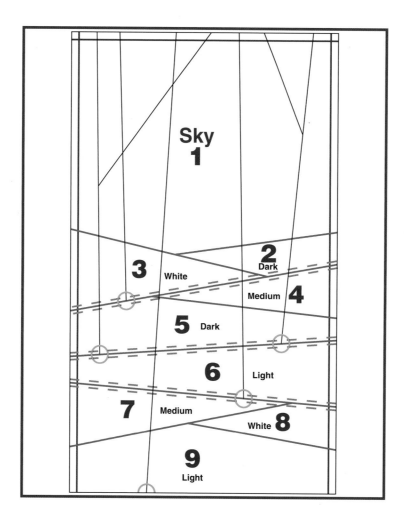

YELLOW CAUTION: ADD FABRIC TO THIS SIDE

It is now time to use the YELLOW colored pencil. At the right-hand side of the pattern, find the first blue/orange dashed section line. From this section line down to the bottom of the pattern, color in the margin between the outside edge of the pattern and the RED "STAY ON GRAIN" line. This step will also need to be repeated in the margin on the left side of the pattern. After this step is completed, write the word: ADD_____" in the yellow margin space of each of these pattern pieces. A total of four times on the left-hand side and five times on the right-hand side. Later in the construction, this space will be used to write the measurement needed to be added to each side of the pattern piece to obtain a consistent size to the quilt top. This is a reminder to measure and add the extra fabric to the sides when cutting these pieces. Every time a suggested tree is inserted it will make the quilt top a little wider. A small amount of fabric will be needed on the sides of these pattern pieces after the trees are inserted.

The RED "STAY ON GRAIN" line at the top and sides of the patterns edge will also need attention every time a pattern piece is placed onto the fabrics.

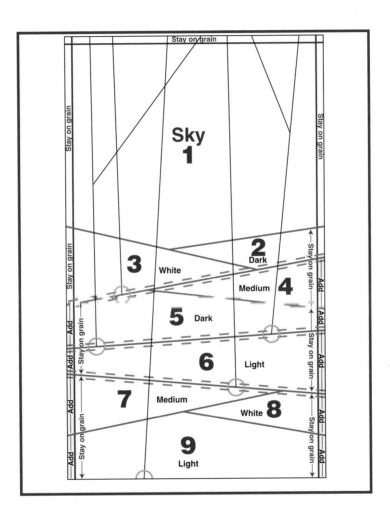

ADDING SEAM ALLOWANCE

At every angle and on both sides of every blue/orange dashed line and solid blue line, add the letters A S A for the words Add Seam Allowance. At least 1/4" seam allowance needs to be added to each pattern piece when cutting the fabric. The letters A S A are a reminder to add at least 1/4" seam allowance.

NOTE: If you tend to take a larger seam allowance then 1/4" go ahead and cut the seam allowances a little on the generous side. Just be consistent throughout this project.

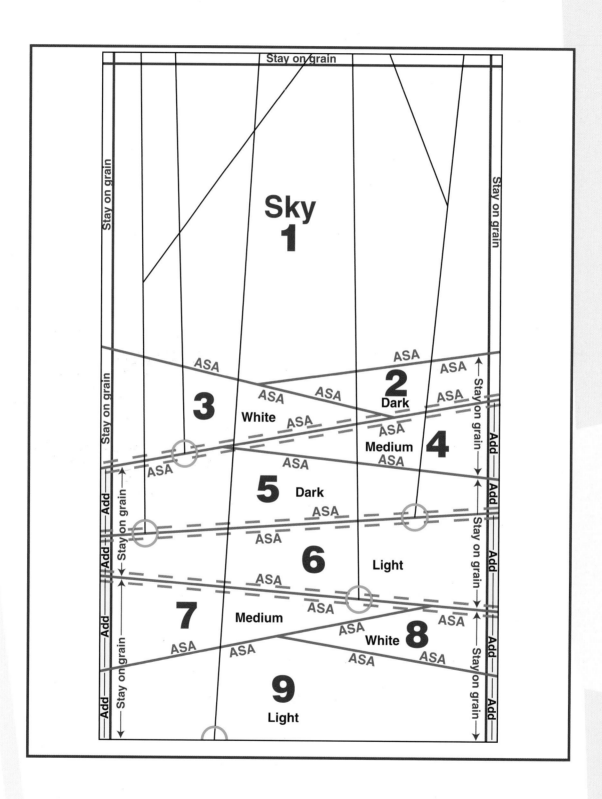

Making the Winter Trees Project

The way this pattern will be used may be just a little different from what you have become accustomed to in the past. Not only will this pattern help call attention to stay on grain, to Add Seam Allowances and remind to ADD_____" fabric at the sides, it will also be used as a placement guide when marking the quilt top for the suggested trees. Working with one section at a time, the pattern pieces are pressed to the right side or front of the fabrics. Small changes and adjustments will be made with tree placement and shifts in the horizon line. These are only a few of the ways, including the way the quilt top is constructed, that makes this technique different from others. This technique will afford so much more freedom with the work on the project. Each time this pattern is reused a different quilt can be created just by making fabric changes, moving a suggested tree or adjusting the shift of the horizon line.

MAKING THE CUT

Start by placing the full pattern on the large cutting mat. Find the first section line down from the top of the pattern. This will be the first blue/orange dashed line between pattern pieces # 3 and # 4. With the ruler aligned with this angle and using the rotary cutter, cut along this line. Place the rest of the pattern in a safe place away from all of the work to be done with this first section.

It is important to work with only one section at a time. Again at the cutting mat using the ruler and rotary cutter, make the cut to separate pattern piece # 3 and # 2 from the # 1 Sky piece. These three pattern pieces are now ready to be pressed onto the right side of appropriate fabrics. Be sure your Sky, dark and white fabrics are pressed and ready for the next step.

IMPORTANT NOTE: Do not cut apart the pattern pieces on any of the black suggested tree or branch lines. These black lines are only used as guides for placement of suggested trees or branches and the pattern is not cut on these lines.

You will be pressing each pattern piece onto the right side or front of the fabrics chosen for your Winter Trees project. With the Sky fabric right side up and pressed flat on the ironing board, place the # 1 Sky pattern piece over the fabric. Adjust this pattern piece to make sure that the grain of the fabric aligns with the sides of the pattern piece and the RED "STAY ON GRAIN" line. Also keep in mind the A S A at the bottom of this pattern piece. Make sure to leave enough fabric for your seam allowance. Press the Sky pattern piece onto the fabric and set it on the table to cool while preparing the next two pieces.

With the dark fabric pressed and ready at the ironing station, place the # 2 pattern piece on the fabric. Adjust the right-hand side of the pattern piece with the RED "STAY ON GRAIN" line along the grain of the fabric. Be careful, this side is only about 2" along the right-hand side and will need close attention to the placement. This pattern piece has three angles to Add Seam Allowance to so be sure the placement will accommodate this. Press into place. Set this aside to cool on the table.

Take the # 3 pattern piece to the crisply-pressed white fabric on the ironing board. Place the left side of the pattern piece in line with the grain of the fabric with enough fabric above and below for the seam allowance, press the pattern piece into place. Set this on the table to cool.

NOTE: Before making any cuts check that the RED line is indeed on grain with the fabric. If not, peel off the pattern piece, reposition and repress onto the fabric.

CUTTING THE A S A

It is now time to trim down the fabric around the pattern pieces leaving the appropriate seam allowance needed. As discussed before, a 1/4" seam allowance is the objective. But, if you know that you take a larger allowance than 1/4", go ahead and cut it a little on the generous side. Just be consistent through out the entire project. We are talking about a fraction of an inch. Only the blue/orange dashed lines and solid blue lines need to have your seam allowance added. OK, make the cuts!

MAKING YOUR MARK

After all three of the pattern pieces for the first section have been cut with the seam allowance added, it is time to mark the placement points in the seam allowance of these pieces. These placement points will help with matching up the pattern pieces when preparing to pin and sew them together. The bottom of the # 1 Sky pattern piece comes to a wide "V ". Make a chalk placement dot with the pink chalk pencil at the point of this V. Pattern piece # 2 has two points to mark for placement, the first dot is all the way to the left side and the second is almost mid-way at the bottom edge of the pattern piece. Mark both of these with the pink chalk pencil. The # 3 pattern piece has one placement dot at the right side to mark.

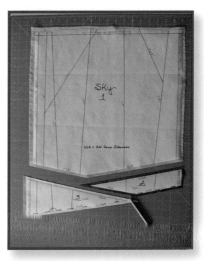

READY TO SEW AND PRESS

Peel off the paper pattern from the # 1 Sky and the # 2 land fabric pieces. Line up these pieces along the corresponding seam allowance edges being sure to match the placement dots marked with the pink chalk. Pin along the seam allowance and sew the seam. After the seam has been sewn and you are happy with the placement, it's time to press. Place this with the front of the Sky and the back of the dark land (# 2 piece) facing up on the ironing board, press this seam as is to set the stitches. Spray lightly with the spray starch and press the seam again. When cool enough to handle, lift the dark land (# 2 piece) and smooth it down towards you with your hand. Iron this down so the seam is crisp and without a pleat. Pressing/ironing in this fashion, allows all seam allowances to be pressed downward.

As with the first two pieces, the # 3 snow piece will need to be matched up with the chalk placement dots in the seam allowance. Pin this together to prepare to sew the seam. After sewing the seam and if you are happy with the placement, press to set the seam, give it a light spray of starch and press again. When it is cool enough to handle, iron it down with no pleat using the same pressing/ironing process used for the first seam. Let this section cool at the ironing station.

CUTTING THE TREE FABRIC

At the cutting station prepare to cut the 2/3 yard of the very dark tree fabric. Fold the tree fabric in half meeting the selvage edges. Place it on the cutting mat with the selvage edges at the top and away from you. Smooth the fold with your hands. Take this folded edge up to meet the selvage edge. Be sure the fabric is carefully lined up, then smooth this fold. By folding the fabric this way, the strips will have a length of 44" and will not have to be pieced together for the trees. Working at the left-hand side of the fabric and off the last fold (the fold that is closest to you), line up the ruler with the fold and make a straight cut at a right angle to this fold. This straight cut edge will be used to measure from and cut the following tree strips. Cut two strips at 1 1/2" wide, two strips at 2" wide and one strip at 2 1/2" wide. Set the remainder of this very dark fabric aside to be used for the binding.

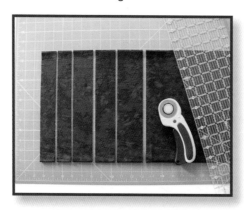

MARKING AND CUTTING
FOR A SUGGESTED TREE

Put the completed first section flat on the work table and lay the three pattern pieces just used in place over the completed work. Notice the top of the root ball at the bottom edge of pattern piece # 3. With the chalk pencil make a reference dot in the seam allowance for the first tree trunk. Follow this line up to the top edge of the work and make a reference dot at that point on the sky fabric. Remove all of the pattern pieces from the quilt top and move the work to the cutting mat. Align the ruler with these two chalk reference dots and, with the rotary cutter, make this cut from the bottom of the piece to the top. After making this cut, the tree is no longer a suggested tree. The tree now has to be planted! Open this cut and place one of the 1 1/2" wide tree strips between the two sides of the quilt top.

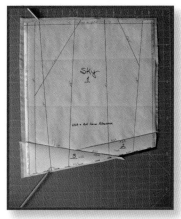
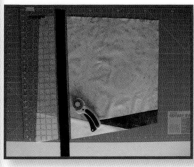

Flip the tree trunk fabric onto the smaller left-hand side of the quilt top with right sides together. Leave about 1/2 " extra tree fabric at the top of the work and pin along the seam allowance. Sew this seam taking care that the seam allowances all stay down on the back of the quilt top. Press to set the seam with the front of the quilt top facing up. Spray lightly with the starch and press again. When cool enough to handle, iron the tree trunk to the right so the seam allowance is under or behind the tree making sure that there are no pleats. Sewing the tree trunk to the narrowest side of the quilt first makes the piece more manageable.

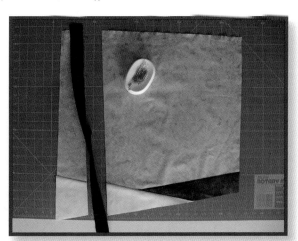

Place the left side of the quilt top on the table next to the right side. This is where you can play with the horizon line. A slight shift up on the left-hand side will give more of a valley in the center of the quilt. Shift the left side up or down until it is pleasing to your eye. Flip the left side onto the right side so they are facing each other. Pin and sew this seam being careful to keep the seam allowances in place. Follow the same pressing and ironing procedure as before making sure the quilt top is flat and without pleats. The seam allowance should be pressed so both sides are behind the tree. Let the work cool enough to be handled.

"TRUE UP" THE BOTTOM

In this step you will "True Up" the bottom of the work to prepare for the addition of the remaining sections. When doing this, you will need to keep the angle and remove the least amount of fabric from the bottom of the work. Place the completed first section flat on the cutting mat along with the unused bottom portion of the pattern. The bottom portion of the pattern is used as a reference for the angle needed for the next section.

If this angle is not cut correctly the next three sections will not fit properly and will not stay on grain. Align the ruler with this angle at the lower edge of the finished section. With the rotary cutter make a cut to "True Up" this angle to prepare the first section for the addition of the next section when it has been completed. The amount of fabric to be removed will vary due to the amount that the left side was shifted when the tree was inserted into the quilt top.

ADDING TO THE SIDES

At the cutting station, put the completed section and the lower part of the pattern on the cutting mat. With the ruler aligned on the next blue/orange dashed line, cut the second section from the pattern with the rotary cutter and put the bottom part of the pattern back into a safe place. Lay the second section at the base of the completed first section. Move it from side to side centering it under the first section. Remember, a tree has been added and by adding the tree it made the quilt top grow one inch wider. With the addition of the first tree, the pattern became a guide and the quilt top will widen with each additional tree. To compensate for the addition of this first tree, some fabric needs to be added to the outside edge of all of the preceding pattern pieces. Adding this small amount of fabric will result in the largest possible quilt top at the end of the project. Measure each side of the pattern to see how much fabric needs to be added to both sides of the pattern pieces. In the YELLOW margin at the right hand side of this section, where you wrote ADD_____", write the measurement of fabric that needs to be added at that side. Be sure to write this on both of the pattern pieces at this side. At the left-hand side write the measurement needed to be added to this side. I added a generous 1/2" to each side but you will need to make your own measurements. Set the first completed section to one side.

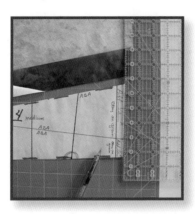

Separate the two pattern pieces in this section by cutting pattern piece # 4 from pattern piece # 5 along the solid blue line with the ruler and rotary cutter.

RED...YELLOW...AND A S A

With the medium color fabric pressed and ready at the ironing station, place pattern piece # 4 on the fabric. Be sure to adjust the right-hand side of the pattern piece with the RED "STAY ON GRAIN" line along the grain of the fabric. YELLOW CAUTION, move the pattern piece to the left to allow enough additional fabric to the right side so that this section will fit with the first section. With pattern piece # 5 use the same attention to detail given to the RED line and YELLOW margin at both sides and iron this to the dark fabric. Cut the A S A seam allowance for both angles of pattern piece # 4 and all three angles of pattern piece # 5 .

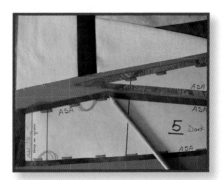

In the seam allowance of piece # 4 make a chalk placement dot at the point that the pattern comes to on the far left-hand side. Another chalk placement dot should be made in the seam allowance of piece # 5 also close to the left-hand side at the highest point. Remove the pattern pieces. After matching the placement dots, pin in the seam allowance and sew the two pieces together. As before, press/iron this section with the seam allowance down and without a pleat on the front.

BRINGING IT ALL BACK TOGETHER

With both the first section and the just-sewn second section on the work table, it is time to sew the two sections together. Slide the sections from side to side until they are aligned. Flip the bottom section up onto the first section with right sides together and pin in place along the seam allowance edge. Sew the seam and press and iron as you did previously for the project.

When the quilt top is cool enough to handle, place it on the work table. Lay all five pattern pieces that have been used in place over the work that has just been finished. Notice, because of the addition of the first tree, lining up these pattern pieces is no longer precise.

Marking For the Next Two Suggested Trees

Adjust the first five pattern pieces as close to the center as possible. Notice at the bottom of pattern piece # 5 there are two green root ball tops. It is time to mark for these two suggested trees. Remember that all of the trees are only suggested until the cut is made in the quilt top. With the pink chalk pencil make a reference dot in the seam allowance at the root ball of both suggested trees. Follow the trunk line of each of the suggested trees to the top of the # 1 Sky pattern piece to make the corresponding reference dots in the seam allowance.

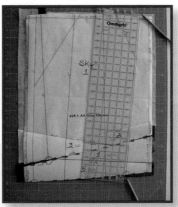

AUDITIONING A TREE

Remove the five pattern pieces from the quilt top and set them to one side. Take one of the 1 1/2" strips of very dark tree fabric and lay it on the right-hand side of the quilt top. Align this strip with the reference dots made for that suggested tree. Do the same at the left side with a 2" strip of very dark tree fabric for the other suggested tree. Stand back a step or two from the work table to see if this placement is pleasing to your eye. If not, adjust either the top or bottom of the strip until you are happy with the look. This is an audition before the actual cut is made in the quilt top. By auditioning the trees, adjustments can be made to the quilt before the cut is made and little changes may be made in the appearance until the desired look is achieved. When you are happy with these two suggested trees be sure the reference dots are correct or make any adjustments before removing the very dark tree fabric strips.

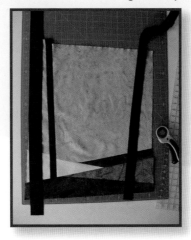

CUTTING FOR A TREE AND BRANCH

The quilt top will be cut for only one tree at a time. At the cutting station, place the quilt top on the cutting mat. Working on the right-hand side of the quilt top, align the ruler with the reference dots for the second tree. Using the rotary cutter, make the cut from bottom to top along this angle and separate the two sides.

Work with the narrow far right-hand side first. Place the 1 1/2" strip of very dark tree fabric face down onto the narrow side lining it up with the fresh cut you just made. Leaving about a 1/2" tail of very dark tree fabric at the top, pin the tree strip into place along the seam allowance and sew the seam. At the ironing station press, spray starch and iron the piece without a pleat. Make sure the seam allowance is ironed to lay behind the tree trunk. Set this side of the quilt top to one side. The tree branch needs to be marked, cut and inserted before the tree trunk is sewn into place.

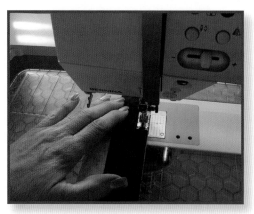

THE BRANCH

Using the # 1 Sky pattern piece, fold the right side back along the line made for the tree trunk. Lay the # 1 Sky pattern piece onto the larger left-hand side of the quilt top lining it up with the cut made for the tree trunk at the right side. Make a reference dot with the pink chalk pencil in the seam allowance at both ends of the line drawn for the branch of the tree. See the photo below.

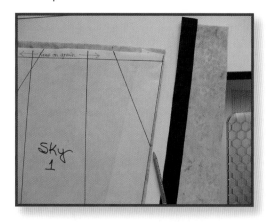

Remove the # 1 Sky pattern piece and place this side of the quilt top on the cutting mat. Line up the ruler with the two reference dots you just made for the branch. Make a cut at this angle and separate these two pieces.

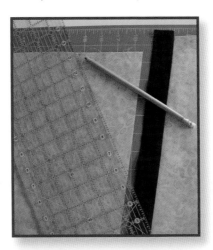

The branch should be narrower than the tree trunk. Use an 11" long piece of the very dark tree fabric left over from the first tree, trim it from the 1 1/2" width to 1". Center the trimmed 11" branch along the last cut of the triangle piece. Flip the branch fabric over onto the triangle, pin and sew in place. Press and iron as before.

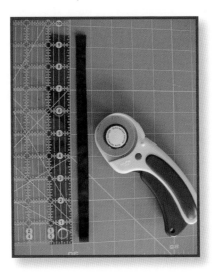

Align the triangle piece at the edge of the large half of the quilt top and pin along the seam allowance. Peek to see if you have aligned this properly. If not, realign until it is correct then sew the seam. Set the seam, press and iron the seam allowance behind the branch.

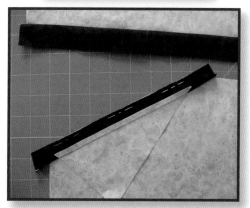

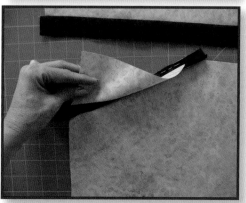

Notice in the photos on page 29, the seam just sewn to insert the tree branch is a little off. To ensure the other half of the quilt will fit properly in place, this side will need to be trimmed. To "true up" this side before the quilt top is sewn back together, place the Sky pattern piece, with the right side still folded back along the tree line, onto the work for reference of the correct angle. At the cutting mat, line up the ruler along the edge at the correct angle. Using the rotary cutter trim the least amount of fabric off without compromising the angle.

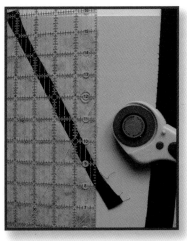

PUTTING IT ALL BACK TOGETHER AGAIN

It is time to put the two sides of the quilt top back together. Decide how much shift up on the right- hand side will be pleasing. This little shift up at both sides of the quilt will create a valley or cradle towards the center of the quilt. The valley will give the viewer a place to be drawn to and will make them wonder what is beyond the horizon. After shifting the right side until it is pleasing, flip the right side onto the left, pin and sew them back together. Set this seam, press, spray with starch and iron in place without a pleat.

Planting the Third Suggested Tree

Working at the cutting station on the left side of the quilt top, prepare to plant the third suggested tree. Align the ruler with the reference dots in the seam allowance at the bottom and top of the work. Make this cut from bottom to top using your rotary cutter. Place a 2" wide strip of the very dark tree fabric between the two sides of the quilt top. Flip the tree fabric face down onto the narrow side lining it up with the fresh cut you just made. Pin in place with about 1/2" tail at the top of the work and sew the seam. After the seam is set, pressed and ironed into place, put this half to one side.

Use the same procedure for the branch on this tree that was used for the tree branch on the other side of the quilt top. Working with the # 1 Sky pattern piece, fold back the left side along the line made for this tree trunk. Lay the # 1 Sky pattern piece onto the larger side of the quilt top and line it up with the cut made for the tree trunk at the left side. Mark a reference dot with the pink chalk pencil in the seam allowance at both ends of the line made for the branch for this tree. Set the # 1 Sky pattern piece aside.

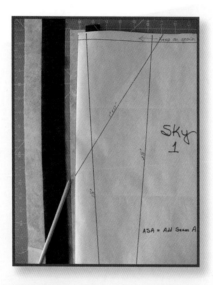

With the large side of the quilt top on the cutting mat, align your ruler with these two "branch" reference dots and make the cut. Use a 17" long piece of the remaining 1 1/2" wide very dark tree fabric and trim it to a width of 1". Center the 1" x 17" strip of tree fabric over the freshly cut side of the triangle piece that was just cut from the quilt top. Pin and carefully sew this seam without stretching the bias triangle piece. Set the seam, press, spray starch and iron the tree branch in place. Line up this triangle piece with the large half of the quilt top. Shift it up or down to be sure this piece will be in the correct place. The alignment of this branch is more important on this side of the quilt because it crosses in front of the first tree that was planted. Flip this branch/triangle piece over onto the large side and pin along the seam allowance. Peek to see if the alignment is correct and make any adjustments necessary before the seam is sewn. It is very important to keep the tree behind this branch looking like it is still connected. When you are happy with the placement, sew the seam. Set the seam, press and iron as before.

After the second branch has been inserted it is time to "true up" this side of the work. At the cutting mat, place the Sky pattern piece over the work and line up the ruler along this edge at the correct angle. Use your rotary cutter to trim the least amount of fabric off this side without compromising the angle.

Find the far left side of the quilt top that has the tree trunk sewn to the right side. Place both sides of the quilt top on the work table. Shift the left-hand side up a little until the look is pleasing. Flip the left side onto the right side, pin and sew this seam. After pressing and ironing this seam into place and it is cool enough to handle, bring the quilt top to the cutting station.

It is time to "true up" the bottom edge of the work before the next section is applied. Place the quilt top on the cutting mat along with the unused bottom portion of the pattern. Adjust both pattern pieces to ensure all parts remain on grain. With the ruler aligned along the correct angle and removing the least amount of fabric, make this cut with the rotary cutter.

Place the pattern onto the cutting mat and using the ruler and the rotary cutter, cut along the next blue/orange dashed line. Notice this section has only one pattern piece. Put the last section back into the safe place. With the quilt top on the work table, center pattern piece # 6 at the bottom of the work. Notice the YELLOW margins on either side of this piece. Keep the section centered at the base of the quilt top and measure from the edge of the pattern to the side of the quilt top on both sides. Write this measurement in the YELLOW ADD_____" margin. I used a measurement of about 1 1/2". Remember to be generous with yourself. At this point you will notice the quilt top has a jagged edge at both sides and the top. This jagged edge is alright, it will be trimmed off after the piece has been quilted. Set the completed portion of the quilt top to one side.

With the light fabric crisply pressed at the ironing station, place pattern piece # 6 on the front of the fabric. As you adjust this pattern piece from side to side check these three things:

A S A has enough fabric for the seam allowance at the top and bottom
RED "STAY ON GRAIN" is lined up with the grain of the fabric
YELLOW ADD_____" has extra fabric at both sides so it will fit the quilt top

After the #6 pattern piece has been placed on the right side of the fabric with enough fabric all of the way around, make sure it is lined up on grain. It is time to iron the pattern piece in place and make the cuts. When the proper cuts have been made remove pattern piece #6 from the fabric and flip onto the quilt top with right sides together. Pin along the seam allowance and sew the seam. Press/iron this seam in place. When the work is cool enough to handle put it on the cutting mat.

Place the #1 sky pattern piece and the #6 pattern piece over the quilt top as close to center as possible. Again, once a tree is inserted, the pattern will not fit exactly any more because the width of the trees make the quilt top wider with each new addition. The used pattern pieces are now placed as reference guides.

With the #1 sky and the #6 pattern pieces centered over the work, mark a reference dot with the pink chalk pencil at the root ball and the top of the next suggested tree. Remove the two pattern pieces. Use a narrow strip of the very dark tree fabric to audition the placement of this suggested tree. Remember that the cut has not yet been made, so you still have the luxury of moving it to the angle and placement that is pleasing to you. Once you are happy with the placement, check the reference dots in the seam allowance at both the top and bottom of the quilt top. Make any needed adjustments to the reference dots. Align the ruler with the reference dots and make the cut from bottom to top for the forth tree.

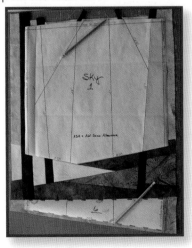

Place a 2" x 44" strip of very dark tree fabric along the newly-cut edge at the narrow right-hand side of the quilt top and flip the tree fabric so right sides are together. Pin together along the cut edge leaving a 1/2" tail at the top. Sew this seam then set the seam and press/iron in place behind the tree trunk. With both sides of the quilt top on the work table, adjust the right side up or down until it is pleasing. Flip the right side onto the larger left side and pin along the seam allowance and sew together. Press/iron the seam allowance toward the tree trunk being sure there is no pleat.

At the cutting station, lay the quilt top on the cutting mat. Put the last unused pattern section at the base of the work as a guide for the angle needed for the next section. It is time again to "true up" the bottom of the quilt top. As before, align the ruler along the bottom of the work. Make any adjustments being careful to remove the least amount of fabric without any compromise to the angle needed for the next section. The amount of fabric to be removed will vary due to how much you shifted the horizon when the trees were inserted into the quilt top.

Prepare the last section by centering it at the bottom of the landscape. Measure both sides to see how much fabric will be needed along each side of the last section. After you have determined the amount of additional fabric needed, write the measurement in the YELLOW ADD_____" margin at both sides of the section. I needed to add about 2" on both sides of my work. After all four of the margins have been marked, cut apart this section into pattern pieces # 7, # 8 and # 9 using the ruler and rotary cutter.

The fabric colors I used for this section are as follows: # 7 medium, # 8 snow white and # 9 light. After pressing these three fabrics, pay close attention to the grain of the fabrics and iron the appropriate pattern piece to the front of the fabrics. Make sure to "stay on grain". Also, allow enough fabric for the Add Seam Allowance and the appropriate amount of additional fabric at the ADD_____" margins. Press into place and when cool enough to handle, make the cuts necessary for each of the pattern pieces. Use the pink chalk pencil to mark the placement dots in the seam allowances at the points on the pattern pieces so this section will match up when pinned together.

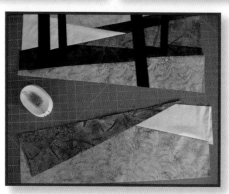

"Y" SEAM

The sewing order for this section will be a little different from previous sections. To avoid a "Y" seam, first remove pattern pieces # 8 and # 9 from the fabric and match the placement dots. Pin, and sew these two pieces together. After the seam is sewn, pressed and ironed with the seam allowance down, pin pattern piece #7 into position matching the placement dots made in the seam allowance. Now sew this seam. Press and iron the seam allowance down without a pleat. The last section has been assembled without a "Y" seam and is now ready to be added to the bottom of the quilt top. Put the upper quilt top sections on the work table and place the section just completed at the bottom. Adjust these two from side to side until they are pleasing. Flip the lower section onto the quilt top and pin in place. Sew, press and iron the seam allowance down.

Now it is time to set in the last suggested tree. Again place the #1 Sky pattern piece along with pattern pieces #7, #8 and #9 onto the quilt top. The last suggested tree runs the full length from top to bottom of the quilt. Make a reference dot at the top and bottom of the quilt top with the pink chalk pencil. Remove all of the pattern pieces and audition for this tree by using a strip of the very dark tree fabric. Step back to see if this angle and placement is agreeable and make any adjustments to the reference dots if needed. At the cutting station, make this cut from the bottom to the top of the work using the ruler and rotary cutter. Separate the two sides and place the 2 1/2" wide tree fabric between them. Flip the strip of tree fabric face down onto the left-hand side of the work with about a 1" tail at the top. Pin the tree in place and sew the seam. Press the seam allowance behind the tree trunk as you have done throughout the project. When this side is cool enough to handle, place both sides together on the work table and shift the left side up or down until the placement is pleasing. Flip the left side onto the larger right side and pin in place. Sew the seam and press the seam allowance to the back of the tree trunk. The Winter Trees quilt top is now finished and ready to be layered with the batting and the backing.

f the addition of another piece of fabric is desired at the bottom of this landscape, the following steps should be taken.

Lay the chosen fabric on the cutting mat keeping in mind the grain of the fabric. Place the bottom edge of the quilt top with about an inch overlap onto the top edge of the fabric to be added.

With the above quilt top and additional fabric on the cutting mat, "true up" the bottom edge of the quilt top. Use the ruler and rotary cutter as if the fabric to be added was not there. Align the ruler to remove the least amount of fabric and keep the correct angle as before. After this cut is made, remove the thin scrap that is left from the bottom of the quilt top and the scrap that is from the top of the new fabric to be added.

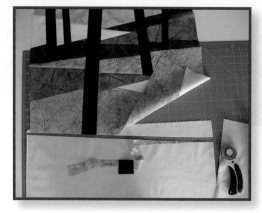

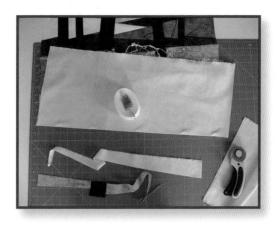

Flip the new fabric up onto the bottom of the quilt top aligning it with the angle just cut. Pin and sew in place and press the seam allowance down. More trees and land may be added until the quilt top is the desired size and ready to be quilted.

THE QUILT SANDWICH

When you are ready to quilt your Winter Trees project do not trim the outside edges until after it has been quilted. To square the quilt top at this time would result in a smaller quilt at the end of the entire process. A little distortion will occur during the quilting process and the quilt would need to be squared up again once it has been quilted because of this distortion. Make the quilt sandwich with the backing, batting and quilt top. Pin with safety pins or baste the sandwich together in preparation for quilting.

I am happy to show a few tips on how I like to machine quilt my landscapes here at home. This is not the only way to quilt this project but I hope you will find one or two of my suggestions appealing. I make a practice sandwich to test a stitch design before putting my quilt under the needle. This helps me decide the movement and texture for each of the different areas to be quilted.

TREES AND BARK

Once you are happy with your practice piece, the first step in the process of quilting your Winter Trees project is to make the quilt as stable as possible by straight stitching on both sides of every tree and branch. This stabilizes the quilt top and contains the quilting areas for a minimum of movement throughout the quilt. After this step is finished, change the machine presser foot to the darning foot for free motion quilting. Quilt the trees using a "bark" looking freeform quilting by moving the quilt up and down within each tree trunk and branch.

SKY

The sky is quilted with free motion curly quilting lines that are flowing and sweeping to fill the area. If a fabric has a cloud-like print in it, those design lines could be followed to emphasize the clouds.

LAND

When quilting the "land," I like to create different textures that show separation between the fabrics used. In the "snow" areas I stitch low sweeping or contour quilting lines as if they are cut fields or low grassy meadows covered with snow. The other areas that are medium or dark fabrics could be tall grasses and brush that would poke up through the shadowy snow within the woods.

Try to stay consistent with the amount of quilting through out the entire quilt. If you began quilting heavily, the entire quilt will look and hang much better if you continue with the same amount or density throughout.

Another option that might be taken advantage of is thread color. The thread color doesn't have to match the color of the fabrics used. The Winter Trees quilt is an ART PIECE and in art not all of the quilting rules have to be followed. By using a variegated thread that ranges from cream to a deep gold, mimicking dead grasses, over the light blue fabric changes the overall look. If a fabric used doesn't quite look the way you envisioned, this is the opportunity to change it. By changing the thread color, you can control shades and hues in the fabric. The depth and added texture the thread colors give, along with the chosen quilting designs used, make the quilt more interesting. If deep blue thread over the light blue fabric is used, an entirely different look will be achieved.

TRIMMING AND BINDING

After all of the quilting has been done I like to wash the quilt to remove any chalk marks as well as the spray starch used while making the project. After you have washed the quilt, lay it flat on a towel to dry and block it if necessary.

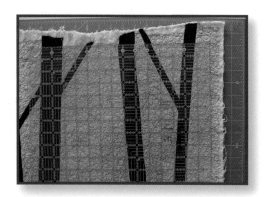

To prepare the quilt for binding, put the dry quilt on the cutting mat at the work table.

Place the 6" x 24" ruler along with a large square ruler on the quilt at the upper right-hand corner. Use the rotary cutter to trim away the least amount of waste while keeping the corner square and in line with the edge of the quilt. All of the cuts made after this corner should be squarely measured off of this first one. Keep the quilt on the cutting mat and turn it to prepare for the next cut. Align the 6" x 24" ruler along one of the freshly cut edges. With the rotary cutter make this cut along the side and proceed in this manner until all sides have been trimmed. Measure across both the top and bottom edges of the quilt to be sure they are the same width. If either measurement differs, trim the quilt until it is straight, keeping the corners square and true. Also, check the measurements at both sides making sure that these too are the same on each side. Trim the sides if needed.

From the remainder of the very dark tree fabric, cut three 2" wide strips to be used for the binding.

Place two strips of the binding at right angles to each other with right sides together. Using the pink chalk pencil draw a diagonal line from the upper left to the lower right corners where the two strips meet. This will be the stitching line.

At the sewing machine join these three strips with a bias seam. Trim the seam allowance to 1/4" and press the seam allowance open.

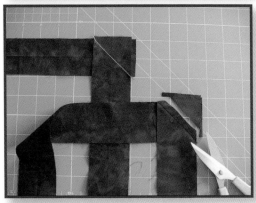

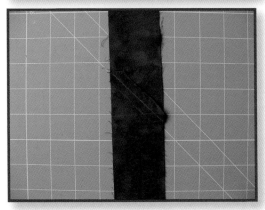

At the ironing station, fold the binding in half along the length of the strip, meeting the raw edges and press to obtain a 1"-wide folded binding. Double thickness binding gives a nice fullness to the finished project and will wear much longer than a single layer of binding fabric.

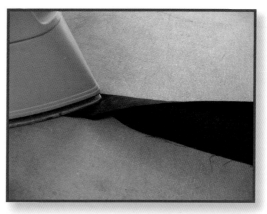

When applying the binding to the edge of the quilt, use a thread color to match or blend with the color of the binding. A 1/4" seam allowance is used to attach the binding.

Leave a tail of at least 6" of binding before placing the edge of the quilt under the presser foot. Starting in the middle on one of the sides of the quilt, sew along the edge stopping 1/4" from the corner of the quilt.

Remove the quilt from the machine. Lay the quilt on the ironing board with the binding you have just sewn running left to right in front of you. Take the long strip of binding and flip it upwards at a right angle. Press in place.

Fold the binding down onto the quilt matching the top edge and the raw edges of the quilt and binding along the right-hand side. Press this last fold.

Take the quilt back to the sewing machine and start sewing the binding on at the edge that the last fold was made.

Continue sewing the binding onto the quilt, always stopping 1/4" from each of the remaining corners. Repeat the steps used to miter the corners. After the binding has been sewn to the last corner, stop sewing about 8" from the starting point. Remove the quilt from the machine and lay it on the ironing board with the opening of the binding ready to be connected. Near the center of the opening where the binding was started and stopped, fold one binding tail at a right angle away from the quilt and the other tail at a right angle over the quilt. With the folds of the right angles butted together, press the binding with the iron. I marked the fold with the pink chalk pencil to keep from losing the correct angle for each tail.

Working with one tail at a time, open the folds of the binding and press it along the last fold made. Press the second tail in the opposite direction to prepare it to be joined to the first.

Mark the newly pressed fold with the pink chalk pencil so it will be easy to match the seam line to be sewn.

Place the folds together and pin. Check to see that the binding has been positioned correctly and will fit the length it needs to cover. Make any necessary adjustments along the inside of the fold line and, if the match is good, go ahead and sew it together. Recheck the seam before trimming the seam allowance.

If sewn correctly and the fit is good, press the seam allowance open, trim, and fold the binding back to its 1" width and press back in place. Sew the remainder of the binding onto the quilt.

After finishing the application of the binding, put the quilt on the ironing board and press the binding out or away from the quilt. This step will ensure a crisp binding line on the front of the quilt. Stitch the binding on the back of the quilt by hand.

The Finishing Touch

It is very important to label the quilt, not only because so much work went into the quilt but so others can identify the quilt. Even if the quilt isn't sent to competitions, it's a good idea to label it. The label should include the name of the maker and the quilter if different from the maker. If you choose, you can add the year the quilt was made and the name of the quilt or pattern used.

The next time the opportunity arises for a quiet walk in the woods, take the time to notice the real colors, varied textures and lovely seasons in nature.

GALLERY

Left: **Winter Trees Table Runner** by Jane Kennedy, 16 1/2" x 58",
adds a bit of moonlight to your dining room even on the darkest of nights.

Right: **Jane's Back Yard,** 18 1/2" x 42" was made by Klonda Holt, Greenwood, Missouri,
while taking a workshop taught by Jane Kennedy at Quilter's Station, Lee's Summit, Missouri.

53

One look at **Allendale Winter** by Sande Wilcher of Lee's Summit, Missouri, is almost enough to make one shiver.
Sande made this 50" x 64" quilt while taking a workshop at Quilter's Station, Lee's Summit, Missouri.

Out on a Limb by Klonda Holt, Greenwood, Missouri,
shows a bright red cardinal stopping by the woods on a snowy evening on this 22" x 34 1/2" wall hanging.

Lavender Moon by Jane Kennedy illustrates the impact small color changes can make.
The wall hanging measures 21 1/2" x 32".

Top: **Come Winter,** 29 1/2" x 25 1/2", illustrates what a bit of "thread painting" can do for a quilt.
Jane Kennedy added small shrubs and grasses using dark thread as she quilted.

Bottom: Jane Kennedy used traditionally pieced maple leaves as a fun background for **Moonlight and Maples.**
The quilt is larger, measuring 67" x 72". Quilting by Beth Kurzava, Raytown, Missouri.

Country Sunshine, 35" x 39" by Klonda Holt, Greenwood, Missouri,
changes the season from winter to summer simply by using different color choices.

Cheri Rabourn of Lee's Summit, Missouri, took a workshop taught by Jane Kennedy at Quilter's Station, Lee's Summit, Missouri, and came up with this fall wall hanging. **Dusk in the Missouri Autumn Sky**, 18" x 38", has silk embroidery elements.

Woods in Spring Time by Joan Ferguson, Warrensburg, Missouri, measures 19 1/2" x 27"
and shows the woods beginning to green up for spring.